Incredible
Mollusks

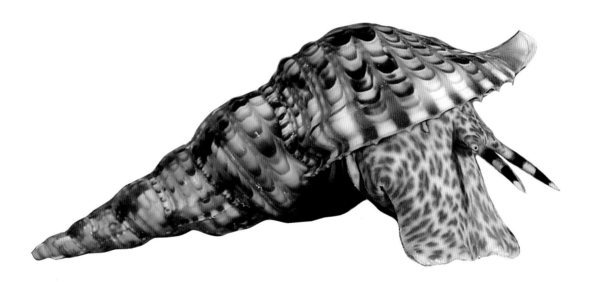

John Townsend

Chicago, Illinois

For information, address the publisher:
Raintree, 100 N. LaSalle, Suite 1200, Chicago, IL 60602
Customer Service: 888-363-4266
Visit our website at www.raintreelibrary.com

Printed and bound in China
09 08 07 06 05
10 9 8 7 6 5 4 3 2 1

Library of Congress Cataloging-in-Publication Data
Townsend, John, 1955-
  Incredible mollusks / John Townsend.
    p. cm. -- (Incredible creatures)
  Includes bibliographical references and index.
  ISBN 1-4109-0528-4 (library binding-hardcover) -- ISBN 1-4109-0852-6 (pbk.)
  1. Mollusks--Juvenile literature. I. Title. II. Series: Townsend, John, 1955- Incredible creatures.
  QL405.2.T68 2005
  594--dc22
                              2004008849

Acknowledgments
The publishers would like to thank the following for permission to reproduce photographs: p. 4 Todd A. Gipstein/Corbis; pp. 5 (top), 42
Lawrence Lawry/NHPA; pp. 5 (middle), 44–45 Karl Switak/NHPA; pp. 5 (left), 10–11, 26 (bottom) F. Bavendam/FLPA; p. 6 (left) Roger
Wilmshurst/FLPA; pp. 6–7, 16–17 Laurie Campbell/NHPA; p. 5 (bottom) G. I. Bernard; p. 6 (left) Paul A. Souders/FLPA; p. 7 (right) Roy
Waller/NHPA; p. 8 (left) John McCammon/Oxford Scientific Films; pp. 8–9, 18 (inset) D. P. Wilson/FLPA; p. 9 (right) E. A. Janes/NHPA;
p. 10 (left) B. Jones & M. Shimlock/Nature Picture Library; p. 11 (right) F. Lanting/Corbis; p. 12 (left) IMAGINA/Astsushi
Tsunoda/Alamy Images; pp. 12–13 A. Wharton/FLPA; p. 13 (right) Pete Atkinson/NHPA; p. 14 (left), 36 (right) Stuart
Westmorland/Corbis; pp. 14–15, p. 15 (right) Matt Bain/NHPA; p. 16 (left) Michael Rose/FLPA; p. 17 (right), 20 (left) Daniel
Heuclin/NHPA; p. 19 Mauro Fermariello/Science Photo Library; p. 18 (main) Peter David/FLPA; pp. 20–21 Jack Jeffrey/Hawaii Photo
Research; p. 21 (right) Clouds Hill Imaging/Science Photo Library; p. 22 Jason Smalley/Nature Photographers; p. 23 (left) Gerard
Lacz/FLPA; p. 23 (right) Tony Hamblin/FLPA; p. 24 Peter Scoones/
Science Photo Library; p. 25 (right) Dietmar Nill/Nature Picture Library; p. 25 (left) Sinclair Stammers/Science Photo Library; pp. 26 (top),
44 (top) ImageQuest 3-D/NHPA; pp. 27, 33 (right) Norbert Wu/NHPA; p. 28 (left) James D. Watt/ImageQuest 3-D; pp. 28–29, 38–39
Jeff Rotman/Nature Picture Library; p. 29 (right) Constantinos Petrinos/Nature Picture Library; pp. 30 (left), 32 (left) Karen Gowlett-
Holmes/Oxford Scientific Films; pp. 30–31 Derek Middleton/FLPA; p. 31 (right) Colin Marshall/FLPA; pp. 32–33 B. Cranston/FLPA; p.
34 (left) B. Jones & M. Shimlock/NHPA; pp. 34–35 Matthew Oldfield/Science Photo Library; p. 35 (right) James Carmichael, Jr./NHPA;
p. 36 (left) Jon Wilson/Science Photo Library; p. 37 Georgette Duowma/Science Photo Library; p. 38 (left) Christine Osborne World
Religions; p. 39 (right) Howard Hall/Oxford Scientific Films; pp. 40 (top), 43 (top) ANT Photo Library/NHPA; pp. 40–41 Norbert
Wu/NHPA; p. 41 (right) Mary Evans Picture Library; p. 43 (bottom) Ron Church/Science Photo Library; p. 45 (right) APHIS/USDA; p.
46 (left) Martin Witherg/FLPA; pp. 46–47 G. I. Bernard/NHPA; p. 47 (right) Peter Steiner/Corbis; p. 49 (left) Araldo de Luca/Corbis; p.
49 (right) Nature Photographers; p. 51 Tim Beddow/Science Photo Library. Cover photograph of a Roman snail reproduced with
permission of Ken Preston-Mafham/Premaphotos Wildlife.

The publishers would like to thank Jon Pearce and Mark Rosenthal for their assistance in the preparation of this book.

Contents

Some words are shown in bold, **like this.** You can find out what they mean by looking in the glossary. You can also look out for them in the "Wild Words" bank at the bottom of each page.

The World of Mollusks

Would you believe it?

- The largest sea snail, found off the coast of Australia, was a trumpet conch nearly 31.5 in. (80 cm) long. It weighed about 40 lb (18 kg).

- The largest land snail is the giant African snail. It can reach almost 12 in. (30 cm) from head to tail. The largest can weigh 2 lb (900 g), and its shell is bigger than a grapefruit.

- In the past, South Pacific islanders used mollusk shells as **currency.**

They are slow, they are quiet, and they are often out of sight. Yet mollusks are everywhere in huge numbers. After insects, mollusks have more **species** than any other group of animals on Earth. Some scientists think there could be more than 100,000 different species. Others think there could be many more still to be discovered.

Mollusks live in a whole range of **habitats.** Most live in the sea, sometimes very deep. Others live in streams or on land, including deserts and mountains. Some scientists think mollusks were among the earliest forms of life on Earth, more than 500 million years ago. For thousands of years they have been important to humans for food, money, and jewelry. The silent world of mollusks still has many surprises.

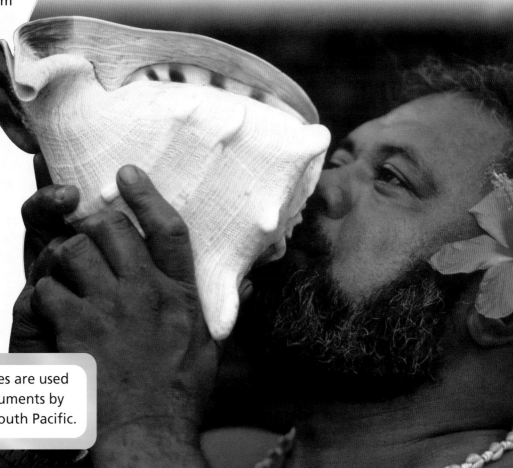

▶ Trumpet conches are used as musical instruments by people in the South Pacific.

habitat   natural home of an animal or plant
invertebrate   animal without a backbone

Find out later . . .

What is special about an oyster's pearl?

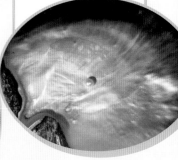

What are the problems with the biggest snail on Earth?

What is so important about mollusk slime?

▲ Octopuses belong to the mollusk group called cephalopods.

What is a mollusk?

Mollusks come in all sizes and shapes. The word *mollusk* comes from the Latin word *mollis*. It simply means "soft." All mollusks have soft bodies, and many have hard shells to protect these soft bodies. They are all **invertebrates,** which means they do not have backbones. Many move around on a flat pad called a foot. Sometimes their heads have bendable **tentacles** for holding food or for feeling.

The three main groups of mollusks are:

- **Gastropods,** which move along on their soft bellies. There may be 60,000 different species, including snails, slugs, and limpets.
- **Bivalves,** with two shells joined at a **hinge.** There may be 10,000 different species, including mussels, clams, and oysters.
- **Cephalopods,** which have tentacles coming from their heads. There may be 650 different species, including squid, octopus, and cuttlefish.

Other groups include sea worms, **chitons,** and tusk shells.

species   type of animal or plant
tentacle   animal body part that is like a long, thin arm

Meet the Family

Long and short

The great gray slug (below) is sometimes 3.9 in. (10 cm) long. It is a European species, but it has been carried around the world on plants and fruit. It is now common in eastern North America. The **native** American slug is much smaller, often less than 1 in. (2.5 cm) long.

Quite often, the bigger species eats all the food. The smallest species then has nothing to eat.

Each mollusk group has some amazing family members.

Gastropods

A **gastropod** is an animal that moves along on its soft belly. The belly is like a foot that slowly **propels** it along. The best known gastropods are slugs and snails.

Many snails have two **tentacles,** like horns. They wave around on top of their heads. These tentacles have eyes on the ends. Snails can be as small as 0.04 in. (0.1 cm) long, but they are usually a few inches long. Land snails like damp places, but they can **adapt** to changes in moisture. Some desert snails can stay sealed in their thick shells for more than a year if there is no rain.

There are also many **species** of sea slugs and snails. These often have bright colors and patterns.

muscular   has strong muscles
native   belonging to that particular place

Limpets and periwinkles

Limpets are mollusks that grip onto rocks so hard that even the most determined **predator** cannot get them off. Limpets are left clinging to rocks when the tide goes out. A limpet has a **muscular** foot that clamps down tightly onto the rock so nothing can pry it off. Rocks are often covered with these clinging shells at low tide. When the tide comes in again, they let go and move over the rocks looking for food. They feed on seaweed.

Periwinkles are sea snails that live on seashores around the world. When a periwinkle hides in its shell, it closes a hard plate behind it to stop anything from getting in to eat it.

Whelks

Whelks are larger than periwinkles, with spiral shells up to 9.4 in. (24 cm) long. They eat other mollusks using long, sharp tongues, as seen below. They poke their tongues into the shells of oysters and mussels. Then they spit an **acid** that breaks down the animal's body, which they slurp up like a milk shake!

◄ This rock pool is full of periwinkles, with a limpet (bottom left).

---

predator   animal that hunts and eats other animals
whelk   sea animal without a spine that has a spiral shell and moves on its belly

Mollusks that ruin boats

Boring clams got their name because they bore, or drill, holes through wood. Shipworms like the one below are actually clams rather than worms. They can do a lot of damage to wooden boats, boring through a thick plank of wood in less than one year.

Bivalves

Bivalves are mollusks with two shells joined by a **hinge.** The two halves are called valves, and they open and close. People eat bivalves as seafood and call them shellfish, although they are not really fish.

Oysters and clams

Oysters often live in groups called oyster beds. Beds of bluepoint oysters are found along the eastern coast of North America. Chesapeake Bay, in the United States, is the largest oyster-producing area in the world. Oysters are unable to move on their own, but they are carried by waves.

Clams are bivalves with thick, heavy, heart-shaped shells.

FAST FACTS

The quahog is an ocean clam named by Native Americans. It can live to be 220 years old.

bivalve   mollusk with two shells joined at a hinge
gland   part of the body that makes hormones and other substances

Mussels, scallops, and cockles

Bivalves often have a fleshy covering along the edge of the shells. Some have waving **tentacles** with tiny eyes on the ends.

There are many different types of mussel, and they are all related to **scallops, cockles,** and oysters. The blue mussel has a blue-black shell up to 4.3 in. (11 cm) long. When the mussel is closed, its large, **muscular** foot is usually the only body part that can be seen. At the end of this foot, there is a **gland** that makes a thread. The mussel uses this thread to move or to cling onto rocks.

There are hundreds of **species** of scallops and cockles, which are similar to clams and oysters. They feed on tiny sea plants and animals.

▶ Mussels hold onto rocks using thin, sticky threads.

Useful shells

- Shells keep mollusks safe. Yet birds such as the oystercatcher above have hard beaks like chisels that can open mussel and oyster shells. They can get inside quickly to scoop out the mollusk.

- Scallops and some other bivalves move by pushing out water. By quickly shutting their shells, they squeeze out water. This **propels** them along like a jet.

propel   drive or push forward
scallop   mollusk with two joined shells that are semicircular with wavy edges

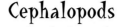

Cephalopods

Cephalopods are different from other mollusks. They still have soft bodies with **tentacles,** but some can move really fast. They often have very long tentacles around their heads.

There are about 650 species of octopus, squid, and cuttlefish. Both octopuses and squid have mouths like parrot beaks, but they have no outside shells. Many **species** live in the deepest parts of the ocean. An octopus has eight tentacles of the same length. It also has a funnel through which water can be squirted to **propel** it along.

The squid has ten tentacles, and two of them are much longer than the others. These are usually pulled back into two pockets near its mouth. The giant squid can weigh up to 4.4 lb (2,000 kg) and is the largest **invertebrate** on Earth.

Many arms

The word *cephalopod* means "head-footed." These mollusks have feet that seem to come out of their heads. All octopuses have eight tentacles, while squid and cuttlefish (shown above) have ten. The nautilus can have 30 to 90 tentacles.

▶ The Maori octopus lives in the sea off Australia.

calcium   mineral that animals need in food for strong bones and teeth
cephalopod ("sef-a-la-pod")   mollusk that has tentacles coming from its head

Cuttlefish

The cuttlefish looks like a small, flattened squid with a fin running around its body. It has a shell-like bone inside its body. The shells of dead cuttlefish (cuttlebones) are often washed up on beaches. These cuttlebones are given to birds, since they are full of **calcium** and are good for parrots to peck.

Some species of cuttlefish swim in groups, and they are found in many tropical waters. The giant cuttlefish is found in the waters off southern Australia. It can reach 3.3 ft (1 m) long and weigh 6.6 lb (3 kg).

Only one type of cephalopod has a spiral shell like other mollusks. This is the nautilus. It swims along the seabed using its tentacles to find **prey**. A nautilus can dive to depths of 1,640 ft (500 m) and travel up to 0.6 mi (1 km) in one day.

A tough life

Eels, sharks, swordfish, penguins, seals, whales, dolphins, and humans are just some of the **predators** that find cephalopods tasty. If they are lucky, octopuses can live for about three years. Larger cephalopods and those in very cold waters may live longer. The giant squid and the giant octopus are thought to live for up to five years.

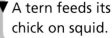

▼ A tern feeds its chick on squid.

prey   animal that is killed and eaten by other animals

Shapes of mollusk shells

- A **gastropod** shell can be shaped like a cap, an ear, a pear, a corkscrew, an egg, or a mixture of all of these.

- A **bivalve** can look like a frisbee, a fan, a triangle, or a long boat, or it can be heart-shaped.

- A tusk shell is shaped like a curved elephant's tusk.

- A chiton is shaped like a shield.

Odds and ends

There are many **species** of mollusks that do not fit into the three main groups. These all have their own special differences. **Chitons** are sometimes called coat of mail shells, since they have eight overlapping shell-plates that look like a suit of armor (or "chain mail"). They have no eyes. There are about 650 different species of this mollusk. The largest can be over 31 in. (80 cm) long. Chitons live in the sea and in rock pools. They press their bodies hard to the ground like limpets and cannot be pried off. They are more active at night, because during the day they tend to cling to the undersides of rocks and ledges. Chitons are **herbivores** and feed on **algae** growing on rocks.

▷▷▷▷▷▷▷▷▷▷▷
To find out more about how mollusks breathe, look at pages 16 and 17.

▲ Here a chiton sticks to a rock with a limpet as a neighbor.

algae   types of simple plant without stems that grow in water or on rocks
chiton ("ky-ton")   mollusk with an oval shell made up of eight overlapping plates

Tusk shells

There are about 350 different species of tusk shells that live in the sea. They burrow into sand and stick up like elephant tusks. They range in size from just 0.08 in. (2 mm) long to 5.9 in. (15 cm). They all feed by spreading their tiny **tentacles** down into the sand.

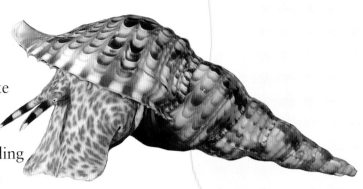

Other mollusks

There are about 250 species of wormlike mollusks, sometimes living at very great depths in the oceans. They have no shell and can grow to 11.8 in. (30 cm) long.

▲ This Triton trumpet shell is one of the biggest sea snails.

Length of largest mollusks (in feet)

Giant squid	55.0
Giant clam	4.59
Australian trumpet	2.62
Hexabranchus	1.72
Steller's coat	1.54
Freshwater mussel	0.98

gastropod invertebrate that moves along on its soft belly
herbivore animal that only eats plants; a vegetarian

Amazing Bodies

U-turn

Some **species** of octopus can leave the water to hunt for food, such as shrimp and other mollusks, in rock pools. The Caribbean reef octopus, like the one below from the Florida Keys, has been seen crawling over rocks and even up walls. It can only stay out of water for a few minutes at a time, since it cannot breathe without lungs.

The **cephalopod** can move in three ways. It can push a jet of water out through a funnel to **propel** it along, it can flap its **tentacles** like wings, and it can walk along the ocean floor. The funnel can turn in any direction, which means the cephalopod can move in any direction. If you want to catch an octopus, your chances are better at night. That is because it moves up to the surface of the sea at night and goes back down at dawn.

The cuttlefish glides through the water by gently rippling its skirtlike fins. It can go up or down by changing the amount of liquid or air inside its bones.

The squid can swim faster than any other **invertebrate** by letting water into its body and squirting it out at high speed.

cockle   sea mollusk that has a ribbed shell composed of two joined parts

Getting around

Some **bivalves**, such as **cockles**, move along the seabed by jumping. Their feet act like springs that keep kicking them forward. Oysters cannot move like this, since they have much smaller feet. They rely on waves and **currents** to carry them.

Scallops swim in jerky movements through the water by slamming their two shells shut. The constant opening and shutting forces out water. This propels them along.

Mussels live glued to rocks, bigger shells, or other mussels. They also cling to piers or sea walls. A **gland** in the mussel's foot makes a fine line of glue that hardens in the water and becomes a strong thread. The mussel holds on and can pull itself along this thread. It can even use this thread to tie up **predators** such as snails.

Moving at the speed of a snail

The common garden snail takes more than three minutes just to move 3.3 ft (1 m). At this rate, it would take over two days to travel 0.6 mi (1 km).

◄ This cockle orb shell is a bivalve mollusk.

---

current   body of water that moves in a particular direction

Keeping alive

All land slugs and snails breathe air using lungs, while all water mollusks take oxygen from the water through gills. Water has to keep passing through the mollusk so that its gills can get oxygen from the water. It then absorbs oxygen into its blood vessels.

Breathing

All animals need **oxygen** to live. They must breathe by taking in oxygen from the surrounding air or water. Blood carries this oxygen to the brain and muscles. Land animals breathe using lungs, while fish and other sea animals breathe with **gills.** The gills are slits that take oxygen from water flowing through them.

So if mollusks get oxygen from water, how do they cope when the tide goes out and they are left high and dry? They must keep wet. Limpets trap a tiny puddle of water in their shells. Keyhole limpets fan this water over their gills and out of the "keyhole" at the top of their shell. Other limpets have gills on the edge of their shells.

▲ The gills of this mussel take food as well as oxygen out of the water.

cilia   tiny hairs that wave together to create movement
gills   flaps that some animals have to breath underwater

Gills

Most **bivalve** mollusks have one pair of long gills. Tiny hairs called **cilia** sweep water over the gills. Bivalves also use their gills to feed; they trap food particles as well as oxygen.

Some mussels live in seawater and others live in freshwater. They all breathe with gills, and some **species** have two openings. Water flows in through one opening and out through the other. This is like breathing in through one nostril and breathing out through the other. They can spend time out of water—they do not have to keep water flowing through them all the time, as fish do.

Surviving

Most water mollusks, like the periwinkles below, can slow down their breathing out of water or when the tide is out. They can manage without oxygen until the tide comes back in. Some species can cope with freezing. Some periwinkles can **survive** in temperatures of –4 °F (–20 °C), with 75 percent of their body water frozen.

▲ Mussels may be left high and dry at low tide.

oxygen   one of the gases in air and water that all living things need
survive   stay alive despite difficulties and dangers

Eyes everywhere

Some members of the scallop family, like the one below, have many eyes. They all help the scallop to see if a **predator** is coming. The eyes look in all directions and give warning signals when danger approaches. This gives the scallop enough time to clam up.

Sight

Although most mollusks have poor vision, **cephalopods** such as squid and octopuses can see well. Cephalopods have the most developed eyes of any **invertebrate.** The eyes of octopuses are as **complex** as those of **mammals** and are similar in many ways to human eyes. They can also turn like ours to look in any direction.

One type of squid has two eyes that are very different from each other. One eye is twice as big as the other and looks like a tube with a yellow **lens.** It seems that the smaller eye is used to look at things close up and on the seabed. The larger eye seems to be used to view the world above. It may also be used to spot the faint lights given off by sea animals in their deep, dark world.

▲ For the size of its head, a squid's eyes are enormous.

adapt   gradually change to fit a particular environment
complex   detailed and complicated

The giant squid is famous for its huge eyes. It has the largest eyes in the animal kingdom. They are **adapted** to see at great depths, where there is little light.

Touch and smell

An octopus has a well-developed sense of touch. The rim of each sucker on its **tentacles** can feel many details. Studies have shown that a blindfolded octopus can tell the difference between objects of various shapes and sizes.

Some **gastropods** have a well-developed sense of smell. They can detect food in the water from a long distance.

▼ This octopus is being tested in a laboratory tank.

lens   clear, curved part of the eye
mammal   warm-blooded animal that has hair and feeds milk to its young

Feeding

Old shells

Mollusks grow their shells by absorbing **calcium** from the food they eat. Tiny shells, bones, and fish contain a lot of calcium. By measuring how much calcium and other minerals are in mollusk shells, scientists can figure out the quality of the water and their **habitat.**

Mollusks are like most other animals in that a lot of their time is spent trying to keep safe, looking for a mate, and searching for food. Eating and finding the next meal can be a life's work.

Finding food

The wolf snail lives on land and tracks down its **prey** by going on the prowl like a wolf! Its favorite food is smaller snails. It finds them by following their trail of slime. Then it chases them. At least, it goes after them two to three times faster than a normal snail. The wolf snail eats tiny snails whole. It turns over larger snails and gets into their shells before eating them alive.

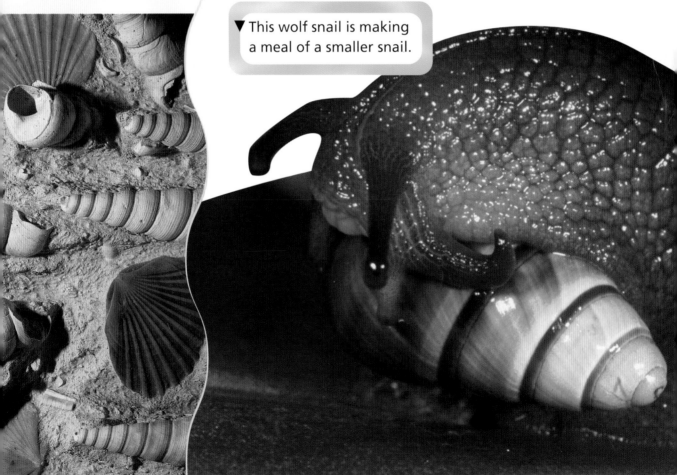

▼ This wolf snail is making a meal of a smaller snail.

acid   liquid that can be strong enough to break down materials

Smart tricks

An octopus finds food such as crabs and other mollusks by using bait. It often attracts its victim by wiggling the tip of a **tentacle** to look like a worm in the sand. Then it sinks its sharp beak into the victim's shell and injects a poison that kills its prey.

The right tool for the job

Many mollusks have a special tongue called a **radula,** which is like a long, rough file covered with tiny teeth. It is just right for poking into other shells or for getting weed out of rock cracks. It is pulled into and out of the mouth with a rough scraping motion. Only mollusks have this tool.

The number of teeth on the radula in different mollusk species varies from a few to many thousands. **Bivalves** are the only mollusks that do not have radulae.

Breaking into shells

Some sea snails are **predators** and use their radulae (shown above) to bore, or drill, holes through the shells of other mollusks. They then suck out the flesh. Some even make an **acid** that can eat through a mollusk's shell.

radula long, rough tongue like a file

Ways of feeding

A large number of mollusks are **herbivores** or grazers, especially the **chitons** and many slugs and snails. Tusk shells feed on tiny bits of material that sink to the seabed. Most **bivalves** filter material and **sediment** from the water.

Herbivores

On land, mollusks are big plant-eaters. Any gardener's biggest enemies are bound to be slugs and snails. They are major pests in farming, since they destroy young plants. Slugs also feed on many fruits and vegetables just before harvest. This feeding may not harm the fruit, but **bacteria** can get into the wounds and ruin the crop. Also, food covered in slime does not look very tasty.

Slugs hide in the day and eat plants at night. They eat small shoots and the edges of bigger leaves. Slugs often climb trees in search of food. To get down again, they drop slowly on a slimy thread. Many birds, badgers, and hedgehogs are natural **predators** of garden slugs.

▼ The slug is plant enemy number one.

anus   opening at the very end of the digestive passage
bacteria   group of tiny creatures that can cause disease

Digestion

Like all animals, mollusks need to get **nutrients** into their bodies. This gives their organs and muscles a regular supply of energy. Plants contain many important nutrients that mollusks need to absorb in their stomachs. Juices and **acids** in their stomachs break down the food so that it can get into the blood. Waste material that cannot be digested goes into the **intestine** and is then passed out through the **anus.** This waste can sometimes be found on lettuce or cabbages.

A slug's **radula** can have as many as 27,000 teeth. They scrape and rub rather than cut and chew like our teeth. Just like sharks, slugs lose and replace their teeth throughout their lives.

▶ Common snails can soon strip a plant with their radulae.

intestine   part of the digestive system after the stomach
sediment   small particles that settle to the bottom of water

Predators

Many mollusks feed on smaller animals such as other tiny mollusks, **crustaceans,** fish, or fish eggs. Some wait for these to drift by before they suck them in, while others go out hunting.

All **cephalopods** are **carnivores.** Like most other mollusks, they have a **radula,** but they also have a pair of powerful, beaklike jaws. These jaws are strong and sharp, so the animal can bite and tear apart food.

Squid often dart up to a fish, grab it with their **tentacles,** and bite a chunk out of its neck. Their tentacles are excellent for catching fish because they are covered in little suction cups. These suckers grip tightly to any surface. Large squid can be difficult to pull off an object to which they want to cling.

Underwater vampire

One sea snail has been called the vampire snail because it feeds on the blood of sleeping parrot fish. It sneaks up on the parrot fish and clings on. It then bites around the fish's mouth and eats its blood.

Here a sea snail is eating coral.

crustacean   sea animal with legs and a hard shell such as crabs, lobsters, and shrimp
host   animal or plant that has another animal or plant living in or on its body

Parasites

A number of mollusks are **parasites.** This means they feed on other living animals. Many mollusks such as sea snails feed on sponges. The **host** sponge is not killed or eaten up completely, but it is damaged. Some sea snails also attach themselves to **coral,** starfish, and sea urchins and eat them.

The **larvae** of freshwater mussels are in danger of being swept away by the flowing water. They could easily be carried out to sea. To solve this problem, larvae of almost all freshwater mussels cling to the gills of fish and **survive** by being parasites. When they are big enough, the young mussels are able to let go of their free ride. They can then live on their own on the riverbed.

▼ The beak of a giant squid can do some real damage to other sea animals.

Swapping roles

Mussel larvae use fish as hosts—but some fish use mussels as hosts! The bitterling (shown above) is a small fish that lays its eggs inside the common pond mussel's shell. The tiny bitterlings hatch and grow inside the mussel, then swim away after a few weeks.

>>>>>>>>>>>>
Find out more about parasite mussel larvae on page 31

larvae   young of an animal that is very different from the adult
parasite   animal or plant that lives in or on another living thing

Breeding

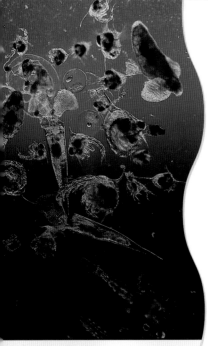

Mollusks have all sorts of ways of making new mollusks. But first they have to meet up.

Meeting and mating

Mollusks are silent, so they rely on sight and scent to find a mate. Land snails and slugs follow slime trails to find each other. **Cephalopods** show off with dancing displays that attract partners. For many octopuses, this is a dance of life and death, since shortly after mating they will die.

Cuttlefish also show off as they gather in large numbers. Rival males wave their **tentacles** at each other and their skin turns bright colors. Then they circle one another and copy each other's moves. The largest and most colorful male wins the female. He keeps waving his tentacles and flashing colors to impress his new partner.

New life

Mollusk eggs are part of the **plankton** floating in the sea. Most mollusks hatch from eggs as tiny **larvae.** They soon settle on the bottom of the ocean or river. Here they mature and grow—if they can escape all the predators. Their shells soon form and protect them from hungry mouths. The plankton above are highly magnified.

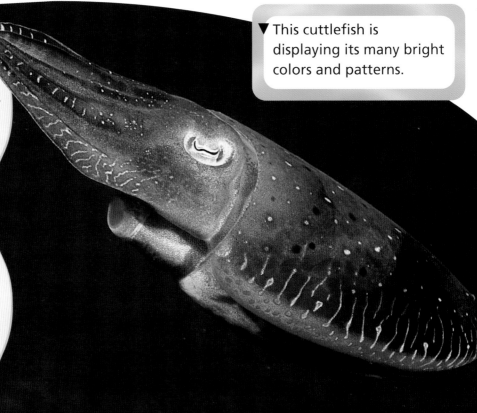

▼ This cuttlefish is displaying its many bright colors and patterns.

fertilize　when a sperm joins an egg to form a new individual
mate　when a male and female animal come together to produce young

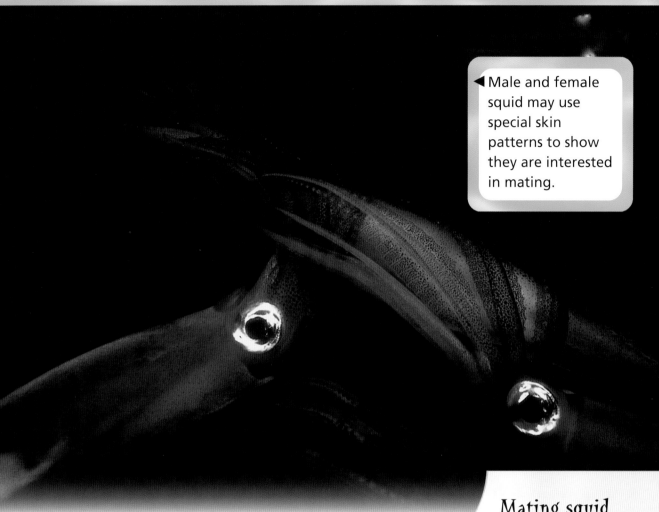

Mating cuttlefish

Cuttlefish lock their tentacles together and **mate** facing each other. The male places a sealed **sperm** packet into a pouch just below the female's mouth. The female then hides in a den, which is usually a deep crack in the rocks. When she is safely inside, she draws each egg out of her body and passes it over the sperm. She lays up to 200 sticky white eggs.

The newly **fertilized** eggs hang from the rock in clusters. Tiny cuttlefish hatch out after four months. The young cuttlefish are just over 0.8 in. (2 cm) long, and many are likely to be eaten by **predators.** Very few of the newly hatched cuttlefish **survive** their first few hours. Those that do survive grow quickly and move to deeper water.

Mating squid

The male squid takes a packet of sperm with one of his tentacles and plants it in the female's **oviduct.** Females then lay eggs, which stick to seaweed or to the seabed. The eggs of deepwater squid are left to drift around in the dark water. Many of them are eaten by fish.

oviduct   tube in females through which the eggs move
sperm   male sex cell

Oyster eggs

Female oysters are champion egg-layers. Some may release over one million eggs in a season. Very few of these eggs will **survive** to become adult oysters. The manta ray below is feeding on **plankton** that includes oyster eggs.

Mating octopuses

When a male octopus is ready to **mate,** he moves close enough to the female to stretch out a **tentacle** and stroke her. His tentacle has a deep groove between the suckers. At the very end of the tentacle there is a spoonlike tip. He puts this under the female's **mantle** and "spoons" the **sperm** into the female's **oviduct.** She then swims off to find a safe den where she can lay her eggs. Sometimes, the male's arm can break off during mating, and it gets stuck inside the female for a while. If this happens, the male simply grows a new one.

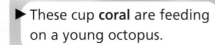

▶ These cup **coral** are feeding on a young octopus.

mantle   fold of skin that covers the body

Eggs

A female octopus can lay 150,000 eggs over two weeks. She attaches them like a bunch of grapes to the roof of her rocky den. She will guard them for the next 50 days. To keep them clean and supplied with **oxygen,** she jets them with water. Then, when they are ready to hatch, she helps the young to escape from their eggs. Not long after her eggs hatch, the female dies. Males die at about the same age as females.

The tiny young octopuses float up to the surface to feed. The few that avoid being eaten soon sink and quickly mature. They then begin their life on the seabed.

Egg champion

Giant clams like the one below can lay hundreds of millions of eggs at once. It may do this every year for 40 years or more. Only a few are ever likely to hatch. The rest become part of the mixture of tiny particles and plankton that many sea animals eat. Some giant clams may live for more than 100 years.

Born in the gills

Some female **bivalves,** such as the ones of the common oyster below, draw in water through their bodies. When this water has sperm in it, fertilization takes place inside the female's shell. The fertilized eggs then develop in the mother's gills.

Larvae

The European oyster and the Olympia oyster do not have to worry about meeting and **mating.** That is because they do it all themselves. Each oyster has both eggs and **sperm.** The eggs are **fertilized** inside the oyster's body and are kept in the **gills** until tiny **larvae** with soft shells are formed.

Bluepoint oysters have separate sexes. Females release millions of eggs into the water, where the males leave their sperm. The larvae develop within six hours and then swim around for two or three weeks. After that, they settle among the stones, shells, and gravel and begin to grow.

Some oysters care for their young inside their own shells until the tiny oysters are released onto the seabed.

nutrients   important substances found in food and needed by the body

Hitching a ride

Tiny freshwater mussel larvae hatch and develop in their mother's gills for a while. But then it is time for a babysitter to take over. When a river trout swims by, the mussel lets her larvae go. The tiny mussels float up to the fish and cling on. They have little hooks to latch onto their new **host**.

The larvae live in their host's gills, where they can filter the water flowing through for **oxygen** and **nutrients**. They also feed off the fish's body fluids. A tiny sac grows around them to keep them safe for what could be a few months. The fish does not have much choice, but the larvae do not seem to harm it, unless lots of tiny mussels clog up its gills.

Life and death

Young cuttlefish are able to breed by the time they are two years old. After laying their eggs (shown above), the females lose strength and their bodies quickly close down. Their lives soon end and they never see their own young.

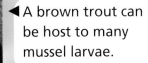

◀ A brown trout can be host to many mussel larvae.

Defense

Eat me if you dare

Bright colors can be a warning to predators to keep away. Some mollusks have a painful sting, and looking scary can save them from being attacked. Others decorate themselves with other shells, pebbles, or pieces of coral or weeds so they cannot be seen.

The chance of a young mollusk making it to old age is slim. All mollusks have soft, moist bodies without bones. It is as though they are asking to be eaten. But they are not all easy targets. Many try to defend themselves.

Color and camouflage

Predators are always on the lookout for a soft snack. But if no one can see a mollusk, it is likely to **survive** longer. So the trick is to disappear.

Many **cephalopods** are masters of **disguise**. They can change their colors and shapes to blend in with their surroundings. Not only that, they can make patterns to help their **camouflage**. Some cephalopods flash four or five different patterns. This is enough to confuse or even **hypnotize** a predator for a few seconds—while the mollusk makes a quick getaway.

▲ A king scallop buries itself in the sand.

camouflage   color or pattern that matches the background
disguise   change of appearance to look different

Extra powers

A cuttlefish can change color in an instant. Even if it is put on top of different designs such as straight lines, zigzags, or check patterns, it is able to copy them exactly.

Some cuttlefish and many squid can glow in different colors. It is thought that about 80 percent of all **species** living in the deep sea can make a special energy in their body cells that makes them glow with their own light. This serves two purposes. The light is a form of camouflage that breaks up the shape of their outline. This makes it difficult for a predator below to see the mollusk's shape against the surface light. The light may also attract mates.

Loud colors

Some sea slugs are brightly colored to trick predators. A good example is this Spanish dancer, which only displays the brilliant red and white pattern on the side of its **mantle** when it is disturbed.

◀ The reef squid lives in the Bahamas.

Pretty poison

Some tropical sea slugs warn **predators** that they are bad to eat. They come in many bright colors to warn they are filled with poison. If they are red with yellow **gills,** like the one below, they say to any enemy, "Bite me if you dare . . . but it is the last thing you will do."

Poison mollusks

Some of the smallest animals can pack the biggest punches. Two types of blue-ringed octopus are among the world's deadliest sea animals. They might look good to eat, but they can kill you. They are found in rock pools around the coast of Australia. Although they are never bigger than 7.9 in. (20 cm) from the tip of one **tentacle** to another, they can kill quickly. The poison found in their **saliva** is so strong that just one of these octopuses could kill 26 humans in minutes.

Blue-ringed octopuses do not usually bother humans unless we pick them up or tease them. They normally look brown or yellow, but their blue rings appear when they are about to attack.

antidote   medicine to make a poison safe
paralyze   stun an animal so that it is unable to move

Deadly

If a blue-ringed octopus strikes, it is hard to tell at first. You cannot tell you have been bitten immediately, since there is no pain. But after just a few minutes you will feel sick and dizzy. Then the poison affects your senses and you lose your sight and sense of touch. Within a few more minutes the poison will **paralyze** you, and it will be hard to breathe and swallow.

The only treatment is to get medical help fast to keep your heart and lungs working. The poison has to work its way out of your system. There is no **antidote.** People have only **survived** when they have had quick medical help. So it is best not to mess with this deadly mollusk—which can even bite through a wet suit.

Deadly shells

They look harmless, but cone shells like the one above have tiny teeth like darts. They fire these at their **prey**. The darts inject strong **venom** that can even kill humans.

◀ The small blue-ringed octopus can kill a human within an hour.

---

saliva   juices made in the mouth to help chewing and digestion
venom   poison

Special tricks

One of the best defense tricks is to make a smoke screen to hide behind. Underwater, it has to be an ink screen. Many **cephalopods** are able to squirt black ink to confuse enemies. Jets of ink cloud the water and allow a cephalopod to change direction as well as color. Then it can escape while the inky water blocks the **predator's** view. Larger cephalopods do not tend to use ink as much as smaller ones.

The ink comes from a special sac that starts to work as soon as a young cephalopod hatches. However, those that live far down in the deep ocean do not have ink sacs, since they would be useless where the water is so dark.

Armor

Most mollusks that surround themselves in tough shells have an excellent defense. Sea snails like the one above can quickly retreat into their armor-plated homes. Spikes and teeth at the shell mouth can stop predators from getting inside. Some sea snails can also produce an ink cloud when in danger. People have used this ink as a purple dye.

► A giant octopus squirts a cloud of ink to keep a diver away.

mimic   someone who acts and pretends to be someone else

▼ This octopus is making itself look like a fierce lionfish.

A good actor

One type of octopus is a skillful copycat. It is called a **mimic** octopus and it lives near the mouths of rivers in Indonesia. It was only discovered in 1998 when scientists saw it "acting." This octopus can turn into the shape of other animals to make its predators think that it is deadly. It can swim by waving its body just like a flatfish. This is probably to mimic soles, which have poisonous **glands.** It also pretends to be a lionfish or may try to look like the poisonous banded sea snake. To do this, the octopus buries six of its 23.6-in. (60-cm) long tentacles in the sand. Then it points just two **tentacles** in opposite directions and waves them, just like the movements of a snake.

Can you believe it?

The mimic octopus has been seen trying to behave like sand anemones and large jellyfish. Predators will not touch these creatures because of their **venom**. You cannot blame the octopus for trying to look scary.

Weird and Wonderful

Disappearing giant

Giant clams are now an **endangered** species. They have been harvested for their meat, shells, and to supply the aquarium business, since they look beautiful in tanks. Clam farms in Fiji are now trying to build up stocks of these rare mollusks.

Some of the bigger mollusks are incredible animals. For years these giants have amazed us.

Giant octopuses

The giant octopus is the largest **species** of octopus in the world. Although it is very unusual to find one over 99 lb (45 kg), now and then some huge ones appear. In 1967 one was caught near Victoria in British Columbia, Canada. It weighed 154.3 lb (70 kg) and was 26.4 ft (7.5 m) from one **tentacle** tip to another. Another was caught off the coast of New Zealand in 2002 and weighed 165.3 lb (75 kg). There are other records of giant octopuses that weighed as much as 401 lb (182 kg).

From time to time, strange mounds of rubbery flesh wash up on beaches. Some people think these could be the remains of huge octopuses.

endangered   at risk of disappearing forever

Massive mollusks

Although there have been a few reports of giant octopuses attacking humans, nothing has been proved. Nor have the stories of human-eating clams. The giant clam has always been of interest to deep-sea divers. The largest known **bivalve** mollusk was a giant clam that weighed an amazing 734 lb (333 kg). It was 4.6 ft (1.4 m) wide.

This mollusk often gapes open like a large mouth waiting for small sea animals to swim inside. Then it closes and slowly digests its food. But a giant clam could only trap deep-sea divers if they were very slow. Clamping onto someone's feet would take awhile, since clams close slowly.

The shells of this mollusk have been used as **fonts** in many churches.

The biggest bivalve

Giant clams are found in the shallow waters of the Pacific Ocean, from Thailand and Japan to Australia. Adult giant clams are unable to move from their position on the coral reef. They stay in one place all their lives and suck in **plankton** for food.

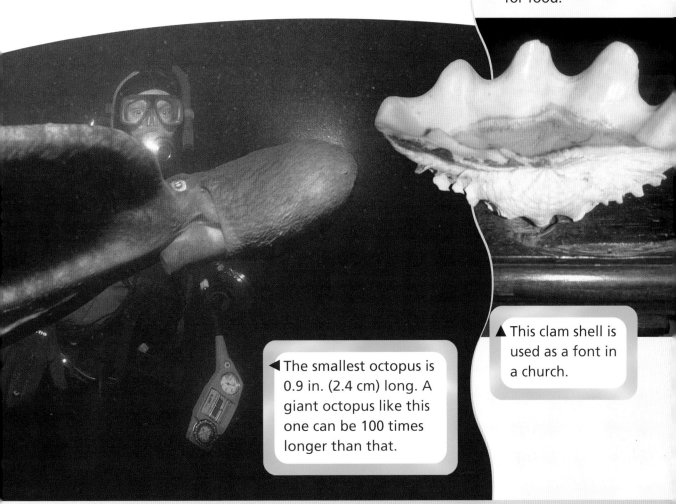

The smallest octopus is 0.9 in. (2.4 cm) long. A giant octopus like this one can be 100 times longer than that.

▲ This clam shell is used as a font in a church.

font   basin to hold water; it is used to baptize babies in religious ceremonies

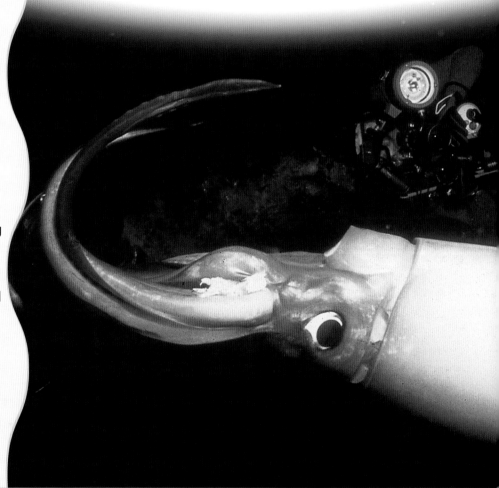

Giant squid

Far below the surface of the ocean lives a huge mollusk that few people have seen alive. Scientists travel down to the darkest depths of the ocean hoping to glimpse one of the most mysterious animals on Earth: the giant squid.

▲ A sperm whale may be no match against a giant squid.

Now and then this largest **invertebrate** of all time gets tangled in fishing gear and is dragged to shore. No giant squid has ever **survived** being caught. But they are out there in the deepest sea, and some are enormous.

The largest of these squid was washed ashore on a New Zealand beach near Wellington in 1887. Its tentacles were about 59 ft (18 m) long and its body was about 6.6 ft (2 m) long.

Fight to the death

In October 1966 two lighthouse keepers at Danger Point, South Africa, watched a baby sperm whale being attacked by a giant squid. They said, "The whale could only stay down for ten minutes, then had to come up for air. It just had time to spout for a few seconds before being pulled down again."

The squid finally won the contest, and the baby whale was never seen again.

legend   old story based on some truth

Squid stories

Giant squid have sharp beaks that have been found in the stomachs of sperm whales. Sailors have sometimes seen whales and squid in fierce battles. It is thought that a giant squid can kill a huge whale. Whales have been found covered in marks from a squid's suckers.

Humans do not often meet up with giant squid. At least one report from World War II tells of survivors from a sunken ship being attacked by a giant squid that ate one of them.

Scientists have demonstrated that the blood of a giant squid does not carry **oxygen** very well in warm water. A squid might **suffocate** in warm water near the ocean surface. If so, it is hardly surprising they are so rarely seen.

True or false?

Maybe even larger squid lurk far below the ocean. Stories of huge squid have been the subject of **legends** for years. The famous sea monster named Kraken, reported in age-old tales, may well have links to giant squid. This huge beast was said to wrap its arms around ships and sink them.

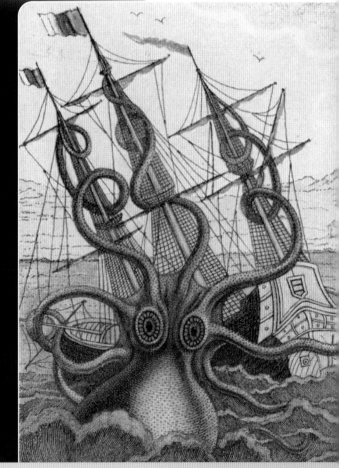

▼ Humboldt squid like this can grow to almost 16.4 ft (5 m) long, but they are tiny compared to their cousins.

suffocate   choke or die from being unable to breathe

How to make a pearl

An oyster makes a smooth substance called **mother-of-pearl** to coat anything that gets into its shell. It is made of minerals and proteins, and it is the same material that coats the inside of its shell. It helps to keep its world silky smooth. It also makes pearls.

Giant pearls

Most mollusks with shells that live in water are able to make pearls. When grit or other material get into a mollusk's shell, it coats it with a substance similar to its shell lining to make it smooth. Some mollusks can grow pearls as big as golf balls.

It takes an oyster about two years to grow a pearl big enough to be used as jewelry. The older and bigger the pearl, the more valuable it is. Pearls from mollusks that do not normally produce them are particularly valuable. A large pearl from a pink conch sold for over $4,000 in 1999.

Pearls come in many colors, including white, pink, silver, cream, gold, and black. Pearls with pinkish-white or pinkish-silver colors have always been the most highly prized.

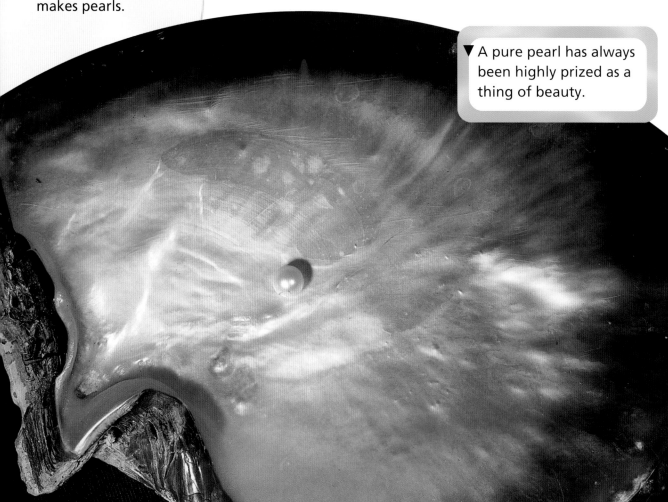

▼ A pure pearl has always been highly prized as a thing of beauty.

mother-of-pearl   substance made by mollusks to coat the inside of their shells

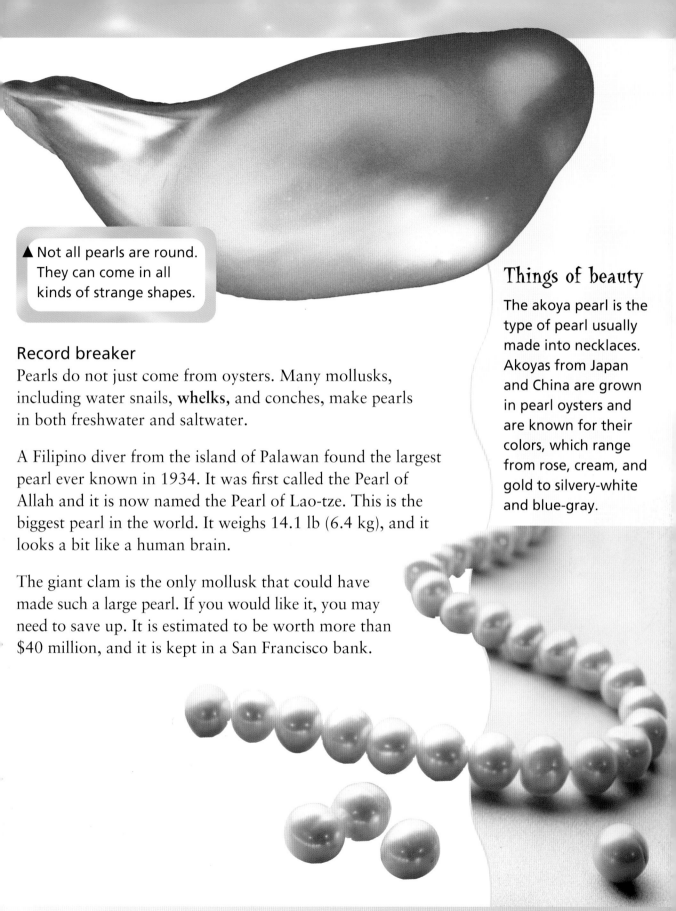

▲ Not all pearls are round. They can come in all kinds of strange shapes.

Record breaker

Pearls do not just come from oysters. Many mollusks, including water snails, **whelks,** and conches, make pearls in both freshwater and saltwater.

A Filipino diver from the island of Palawan found the largest pearl ever known in 1934. It was first called the Pearl of Allah and it is now named the Pearl of Lao-tze. This is the biggest pearl in the world. It weighs 14.1 lb (6.4 kg), and it looks a bit like a human brain.

The giant clam is the only mollusk that could have made such a large pearl. If you would like it, you may need to save up. It is estimated to be worth more than $40 million, and it is kept in a San Francisco bank.

Things of beauty

The akoya pearl is the type of pearl usually made into necklaces. Akoyas from Japan and China are grown in pearl oysters and are known for their colors, which range from rose, cream, and gold to silvery-white and blue-gray.

Giant snail

Scientists think the giant African snail is one of the most damaging land snails in the world. It comes from East Africa, but it is now found in Asia, Hawaii, and sometimes Australia. It can eat through crops really fast.

You cannot blame the giant African snail. It was very happy munching grass in Africa until people thought it would make a nice pet. So the giant snail began to appear in other countries and take over.

A boy returned to Miami from Hawaii in 1966 with three pet giant African snails. He let them go, and seven years later more than 18,000 snails were found, along with masses of eggs. It took the state of Florida ten years and a lot of money to get rid of this pest.

Largest sea snails (length in inches)

Australian trumpet 31.5 (80 cm)

Horse conch 22.8 (58 cm)

Baler shell (above) 18.9 (48 cm)

Triton trumpet 18.9 (48 cm)

hibernate "close down" the body and rest when it is too cold or dry

Threat

So far, the United States and Australia have kept the giant snail under control. But if it gets strong again, millions of dollars of food could be at risk.

This snail is tough. It can **survive** the cold—even snow. It simply slows down and **hibernates** until warm weather returns. So it could survive almost anywhere across the United States. It also breeds in bulk. After a single **mating,** both males and females lay a batch of 100 to 400 eggs. They can do this several times without mating again. In one year, each adult lays about 1,200 eggs. Giant African snails can live as long as nine years, and that is enough time to make thousands of new snails. No wonder farmers must keep on the look-out for them.

Would you believe it?

The giant African snail is known to eat at least 500 different types of plants. Crops of cocoa, peanuts, rubber, beans, peas, cucumbers, and melons can soon be destroyed by a few of these hungry mollusks. The poster below is to make people aware of the damage these snails can cause.

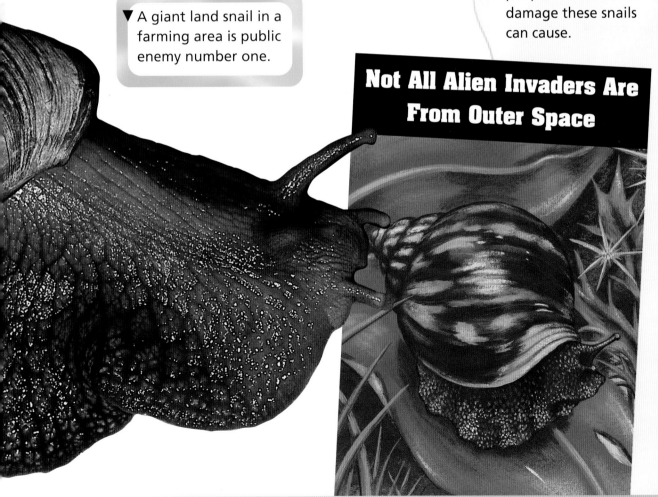

▼ A giant land snail in a farming area is public enemy number one.

Not All Alien Invaders Are From Outer Space

The wonderful world of slime

If you are a mollusk, it is very useful to be able to ooze lots of slime whenever you want. You can slip away from anyone's grip. You can easily slide through narrow gaps. Slime is good for escaping and moving.

Slugs use slime for suction power when they travel upside down. They can then climb up trees, walls, and even windows. Slugs leave a slime trail behind them as they move. This can be useful to let other slugs know where they are. But it can tell **predators** where they are, too.

Slime has a bad name, but it is useful stuff. It is a protective layer that keeps out nasty things—apart from salt. Salt is the one substance with which a slug's slime cannot cope. It makes a slug shrivel up and die.

Slimy friends

Banana slugs like the one above meet and **mate** in a thick goo of slime. Their slime must be delicious, since they often eat each other's slime before mating.

▶ Slug pellets leave behind a shriveled slug and plenty of slime.

   drought   time with no rain and a shortage of water

Slimy

When in danger, a slug is able to ooze a thick **mucus** coating and make its body shorter and fatter. This makes the slug more difficult to eat. The mucus also coats the slug in an unpleasant taste. Slugs can fit into almost any space when they become slimy—long and thin or short and fat. Their slime helps them fit through tight squeezes. They can then avoid sunlight and heat by crawling into small, damp crevices and holes.

Slime also stops a slug's body from drying out. This helps slugs **survive** during times of **drought**. Slugs have been seen eating their own slime trails. It is possible that slime could be healthy to eat—but only if you are a slug!

Slimy and safe

Snails' slime comes out from the front of their bodies and hardens when it comes into contact with air. The snail is able to move on very sharp, pointed needles and over knife blades, razors, rocks, and thorns without getting hurt. The mucus protects its body.

mucus   gummy, wet, and slimy substance made by some plants and animals

Endangered

For all kinds of reasons, many animals are in danger of dying out. Some mollusks are among them. People may sometimes wonder if this matters. What do you think?

Saving snails

Three Australian land snails are listed as endangered. Since 1997 laws have been made to protect their **habitats** with the hope of preventing them from becoming **extinct**. One of these snails is found only in western Sydney. It is called *Meridolum*.

On the brink

The dwarf wedge mussel is a small, yellowish-brown freshwater mussel. It spends most of its time buried in the bottom of streams and rivers. This mussel was once found in fifteen rivers in eastern parts of North America. Its numbers have now dropped, and very few are left. Water **pollution** caused by chemicals used in farming and projects such as the building of golf courses are blamed for the mussel's decline.

So will it make any difference if these mollusks disappear forever? When such **species** disappear, the whole **food chain** can be affected, and other animals may die out or become **endangered.** We should protect our planet's animals for the future.

▼ This woodland habitat in Australia is protected to ensure that snails there do not become extinct.

extinct   died out, never to return
exotic   from strange and unique foreign places

Queen conch

The queen conch was once found from the coasts of the Caribbean and the Bahamas to Florida and Bermuda. This **gastropod** can grow to 11.8 in. (30 cm) long, and it moves by "hopping," using its strong, **muscular** foot to throw itself forward. It may take up to 36 hours for these mollusks to produce up to 500,000 eggs. Today there are very few queen conches left. This species has been overfished for food and for its attractive shell. Such conches were once used as a form of **currency** and were highly prized. They have recently been collected for tourists, since they make **exotic** gifts and decorations for fish tanks and gardens.

Few left

The sandbowl snail, shown below, is very rare. It is a very small snail, less than 0.5 in. (1 cm) long. It lives in damp hollows in sand dunes at just a few sites in the United Kingdom. Its numbers may have fallen because people have destroyed its habitat to develop golf courses or buildings.

▲ This shell has been made into an ornament.

food chain   order in which one living thing feeds on another
pollution   ruining natural things with dangerous chemicals, fumes, or garbage

Medical mollusks

The deadly **venom** of some cone shells is today being used to help victims of **strokes** and heart disease. Scientists may soon produce a new drug from this to help control **chronic** pain.

FAST FACTS

- Snails have been a source of food and protein since Roman times.
- People in France eat 25,000 tons of snails each year.

Mollusks and us

Mollusks matter. They are important to the whole balance of life on our planet. They give us food, but they also have other uses.

More than 1,000 **species** of mollusks have been found deeper than 1 mile (1.6 kilometers) below the surface of the ocean. New species have been discovered since submarines have started to explore the ocean's deepest trenches. We still have much to find out about mollusks. Some may hold answers to all kinds of medical research.

Mollusks are already used in medicine. Ground oyster shells are used as **calcium** to help humans and animals develop strong bones and teeth. Oyster juice has been found to have chemicals that may help fight **viruses**. It might soon be made into useful drugs.

▶ The *Deep Star* research submarine can explore oceans over half a mile deep.

chronic   very severe and long-lasting
stroke   illness caused when the flow of blood to the brain is interrupted

Danger

Mollusks can also bring misery. Snail fever causes great human suffering. This disease is also called bilharzia and affects 200 million people in Asia, the Pacific islands, Africa, the West Indies, and South America. It is caused by the tiny **larvae** of a worm called a schistosome ("shis-ta-soam") that live in water snails. The snails are harmless, but they let these worms **thrive.**

The tiny worms infect humans who wash or paddle in rivers. Within seconds, the **parasites** get through the skin and into the blood. They grow inside blood vessels and the lungs. If they get to the **intestines** or bladder, a victim grows very weak and can die. Destroying the snails is one way of stopping the deadly worms. Drugs can now kill them inside the body.

Mussel power

The threads that some mussels use to attach themselves to rocks are being tested as a possible glue in surgery. These threads are called byssal, which means "fine linen." Perhaps one day mussels may be used to repair muscles!

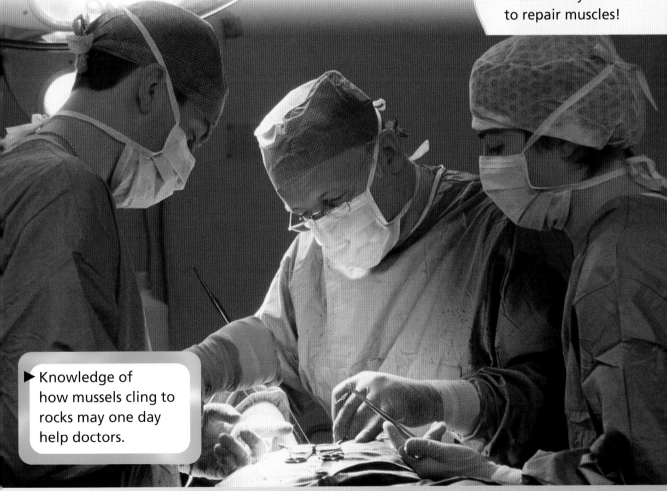

► Knowledge of how mussels cling to rocks may one day help doctors.

thrive   grow with strength and live healthily
virus   organism that causes disease; it is only seen under a microscope

Find Out More

Website

Wonders of the Sea: Mollusks
Website with photos and information about mollusks.
oceanicresearch.org/ mollusk.html

Books

Blaxland, Beth. *Mollusks: Snails, Clams, and Their Relatives*. Langhorne, Penn.: Chelsea House, 2003.

Llewellyn, Claire. *Slugs and Snails*. Danbury, Conn.: Scholastic Library, 2002.

Miller, Ruth. *Mollusks*. Chicago: Raintree, 2004.

World Wide Web

If you want to find out more about mollusks, you can search the Internet using keywords such as these:

- "giant African snail"
- pearl + diving
- "blue-ringed octopus"

You can also find your own keywords by using headings or words from this book. Use the following search tips to help you find the most useful websites.

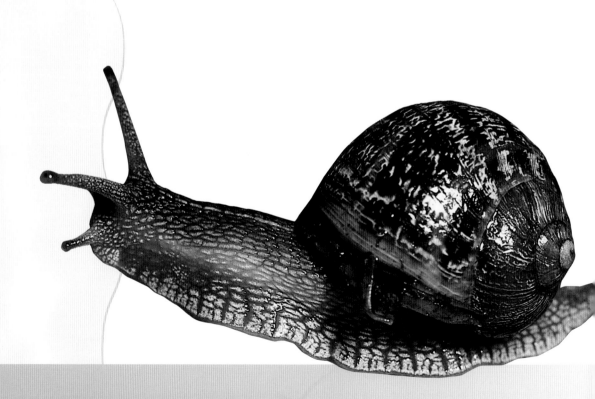

Search tips

There are billions of pages on the Internet, so it can be difficult to find exactly what you want to find. For example, if you just type in "water" on a search engine such as Google, you will get a list of millions of webpages! These search skills will help you find useful websites more quickly:

- Use simple keywords instead of whole sentences.
- Use two to six keywords in a search, putting the most important words first.
- Be precise—only use names of people, places, or things.
- If you want to find words that go together, put quote marks around them.
- Use the advanced section of your search engine.
- Use the "+" sign between keywords to link them.

Where to search

Search engine

A search engine looks through a small proportion of the Web and lists all sites that match the words in the search box. It can give thousands of links, but the best matches are at the top of the list, on the first page. Try www.google.com.

Search directory

A search directory is like a library of websites that have been sorted by a person instead of a computer. You can search by keyword or subject and browse through the different sites like you look through books on a library shelf. A good example is yahooligans.com.

Numbers of incredible creatures

Creatures (y-axis): Amphibians, Mammals, Reptiles, Birds, Fish, Arachnids, Mollusks, Insects

Number of species (approximate) (x-axis): 0, 20,000, 40,000, 60,000, 80,000, 100,000, 120,000, 140,000, 160,000, 180,000, 1,000,000

Glossary

acid liquid that can be strong enough to break down materials

adapt gradually change to fit a particular environment

algae types of simple plant without stems that grow in water or on rocks

antidote medicine to make a poison safe

anus opening at the very end of the digestive passage

bacteria group of tiny creatures that can cause disease

bivalve mollusk with two shells joined at a hinge

calcium mineral that animals need in food for strong bones and teeth

camouflage color or pattern that matches the background

carnivore meat-eater

cephalopod ("sef-a-la-pod") mollusk that has tentacles coming from its head

chiton ("ky-ton") mollusk with an oval shell made up of eight overlapping plates

chronic very severe and long-lasting

cilia tiny hairs that wave together to create movement

cockle sea mollusk that has a ribbed shell composed of two joined parts

complex detailed and complicated

coral tiny sea animals with hard outer casings that live together in large groups

crustacean sea animal with legs and a hard shell such as crabs, lobsters, and shrimp

currency money of an area or goods used for trading and exchange

current body of water that moves in a particular direction

disguise change of appearance to look different

drought time with no rain and a shortage of water

endangered at risk of disappearing forever

exotic from strange and unique foreign places

extinct died out, never to return

ferment when sugars in food turn to alcohol

fertilize when a sperm joins an egg to form a new individual

font basin to hold water; it is used to baptize babies in religious ceremonies

food chain order in which one living thing feeds on another

gastropod invertebrate that moves along on its soft belly

gills flaps that some animals have to breathe underwater

gland part of the body that makes hormones and other substances

habitat natural home of an animal or plant

herbivore animal that only eats plants; a vegetarian

hibernate "close down" the body and rest when it is too cold or dry

hinge movable joint, like the part that fixes a door to a frame but allows it to open and close

host   animal or plant that has another plant or animal living in or on its body

hypnotize   put someone into a trance

intestine   part of the digestive system after the stomach

invertebrate   animal without a backbone

larva (more than one are larvae)   young of an animal that is very different from the adult

legend   old story based on some truth

lens   clear, curved part of the eye

mammal   warm-blooded animal that has hair and feeds milk to its young

mantle   fold of skin that covers the body

mate   when a male and female animal come together to produce young

mimic   someone who acts and pretends to be someone else

mother-of-pearl   substance made by mollusks to coat the inside of their shells

mucus   gummy, wet, and slimy substance made by some plants and animals

muscular   has strong muscles

native   belonging to a particular place

nutrients   important substances found in food and needed by the body

oviduct   tube in females through which the eggs move

oxygen   one of the gases in air and water that all living things need

paralyze   stun an animal so that it is unable to move

parasite   animal or plant that lives in or on another living thing

plankton   tiny plants, eggs, and animals that drift in the sea

pollution   ruining natural things with dangerous chemicals, fumes, or garbage

predator   animal that hunts and eats other animals

prey   animal that is killed and eaten by other animals

propel   drive or push forward

radula   long, rough tongue like a file. More than one radula are radulae.

saliva   juices made in the mouth to help chewing and digestion

scallop   mollusk with two joined shells that are semicircular with wavy edges

sediment   small particles that settle to the bottom of water

species   type of animal or plant

sperm   male sex cell

stroke   illness caused when the flow of blood to the brain is interrupted

suffocate   choke or die from being unable to breathe

survive   stay alive despite difficulties and dangers

tentacle   animal body part that is like a long, thin arm

thrive   grow with strength and live healthily

venom   poison

virus   organism that causes disease; it is only seen under a microscope

whelk   sea animal without a spine that has a spiral shell and moves on its belly

Index